love poems
of alan dugan

love poems
of alan dugan

edited by dan simon

Seven Stories Press
New York ⁂ Oakland ⁂ London

"At Circe's Place" previously appeared in the *Iowa Review* (Summer 1973).

The interview with Alan Dugan by Keith Althaus excerpt, including the poem on Judy Shahn's silkscreen, appeared in *Northwest Review* (1982).

Seven Stories Press
140 Watts Street
New York, NY 10013
www.sevenstories.com

Library of Congress Cataloging-in-Publication Data

Names: Dugan, Alan author | Simon, Daniel, 1957- editor
Title: Love poems / Alan Dugan ; edited by Dan Simon.
Description: New York : Seven Stories Press, [2025] Includes index.
Identifiers: LCCN 2025025708 (print) | LCCN 2025025709 (ebook) | ISBN 9781644215104 trade paperback | ISBN 9781644215111 ebook
Subjects: LCSH: Love poetry, American--20th century | American poetry-- 20th century | LCGFT: Poetry
Classification: LCC PS3554.U33 L68 2025 (print) | LCC PS3554.U33 (ebook)
LC record available at https://lccn.loc.gov/2025025708
LC ebook record available at https://lccn.loc.gov/2025025709

Printed in the USA.

9 8 7 6 5 4 3 2 1

CONTENTS

EDITOR'S NOTE

To give you an idea of just what kind of love poet was Alan Dugan, his own beloved, loving, fellow-creative wife, the painter and printmaker Judy Shahn (daughter of Ben Shahn), always called him by his last name! It was their way, toiling members of the same union, in marriage as it might have been in the IWW.

Dugan was nothing if not a love poet. And the love he celebrated was romantic too, but more a romantic love of today than of yesteryear, a besieged love, eternal even as it was eternally nearly out of gas: crusty, self-effacing, ruthless.

I met Dugan after the great hurricane of him

had subsided somewhat. My friend the poet and librarian Paul Abruzzo had gotten to know Elizabeth McCracken, who was in Dugan's circle. They brought his poems to me. We managed to get rights to his six earlier books reverted by his previous editor and publisher, added his recent work, and brought out the giant collection *Poems Seven: New and Complete Poetry*. New *and* complete. It really was.

The man I met had survived and recovered from throat cancer, the monster that had stalked him. He now drank nothing stronger than O'Doul's nonalcoholic beer. Still tall, fierce, but mildly so, chastened by life and by what had been his approach to it, a different man from what he once was when he was a poet and a drinker. Though I cannot really say since I only knew him in his later years and through the poems.

To prepare the over-four-hundred-page manuscript, Alan Dugan and Judy Shahn convened some of their friends for an exuberant typing and proofing party that lasted for several weeks until it all got done, and I can verify that the manuscript arrived clean and proper. It was dedicated "for Judy." We published *Poems Seven* in early October of 2001, just weeks after the Twin Towers fell. It garnered a front-page review by Robert Pinsky in the *New York Times Book Review*, won that year's National Book Award for Poetry, and went on in its first hardcover edition to sell almost twenty thousand copies that year, nearly unheard of for a book of poems. Miracle upon miracle.

In the grand ballroom of the Marriott Hotel in midtown Manhattan, we milled about in our tuxes, and it turned out that the committee members that were giving him his second National Book Award that night (he also won for his first collection, published in the Yale Younger Poets series for 1961 exactly forty years before!) hadn't heard the news yet that Dugan was now a gentler and quieter version of himself, no longer the guy who would famously excoriate committees for giving him the prize instead of someone more deserving in his view. It was suddenly clear they were still scared of old Dugan, and as he stood up and began to make his way to the podium, someone at the microphone said they were going to spare him having to speak, and that was the end of that.

Something else worth mentioning: Alan Dugan carried a small notebook with him wherever he went, revisiting poems he was writing, keeping them going for months, for years, before he decided one was ready. Considering the spontaneity that always characterized the work he did, it is astonishing that at the same time there was also this sense of caring for them across time and with such patience.

As I reread these love poems, I am struck by the power of reconciliation that informs them—to me it says that you can be hot for your wife and also respect her deeply as an artist, that you need not assume kindness in order to be kind, that you may embody a middle-finger attitude towards everyone and everything, as Dugan seemed to do for so long, and still be a romantic poet and an affectionate child at heart.

A special thanks to the poet of Provincetown Keith Althaus, who back in the early aughts sent me some of Dugan's poems that were not in *Poems Seven* or any other collections, two of which I have included here, along with part of an interview he sent that I transcribed and added as the last word in this volume.

Special thanks also to Tynan Kogane, whose editions of love poems by Catullus and Pablo Neruda at

New Directions were the catalyst and model for the present volume, which grew from a conversation we had at the Pier 42 public tennis courts in New York City in the summer or fall of 2023.

—DAN SIMON
New York City, March 2025

love poems
of alan dugan

ARGUMENT TO LOVE AS A PERSON

The cut rhododendron branches
flowered in our sunless flat.
Don't complain to me, dear,
that I waste your life in poverty:
you and the cuttings prove: Those
that have it in them to be beautiful
flower wherever they are!, although
they are, like everything else, ephemeral.
Freedom is as mortal as tyranny.

(*Poems Two*, 1963)

POEM

A man with a box walked up to a woman with a
     boy, gave the box
to the boy, said, "Don't drop it for a change," and
     kissed
the woman, sucking up her rosebud from her mud-
     color. It bloomed.
He said, "Let's go." They went, with technicolor
     haloes of the usual
around them. Why? Because: They come from a
     star, live by its light,
and burn with it here in the dark outside of the
     department store.

(*Poems Three*, 1967)

POEM

The tree was wet with the moon's
red water when two souls
came down from flight outside the air.

They cried at the fall to flesh
among the snapping dogs on land
and the crawfish in the water

by the tree. Their cries condensed and held
as one dove on and one heart hung
from two different branches. The white dove sang

its love of hearts; the heart
wept blood at its danger. The night
turned blue to be the moon's lungs,
and the red tree its bronchia.

(*Poems Three*, 1967)

LOVE SONG: I AND THOU

Nothing is plumb, level, or square:
    the studs are bowed, the joists
are shaky by nature, no piece fits
    any other piece without a gap
or pinch, and bent nails
    dance all over the surfacing
like maggots. By Christ
    I am no carpenter. I built
the roof for myself, the walls
    for myself, the floors
for myself, and got
    hung up in it myself. I
danced with a purple thumb
    at this house-warming, drunk
with my prime whiskey: rage.
    Oh I spat rage's nails
into the frame-up of my work:
    it held. It settled plumb,
level, solid, square and true
    for that great moment. Then

it screamed and went on through,
    skewing as wrong the other way.
God damned it. This is hell,
    but I planned it, I sawed it,
I nailed it, and I
    will live in it until it kills me.
I can nail my left palm
    to the left-hand crosspiece but
I can't do everything myself.
    I need a hand to nail the right,
a help, a love, a you, a wife.

(*Poems*, 1961)

ON A PROFESSIONAL COUPLE IN A SIDE-SHOW

She is the knife-thrower's lady:
around her outline
there is a rage of knives.
Unharmed, he hopes, inside,
she is love's engine
of dark business
and the target of design.

What does she think of this?
The same, reversed: money is money
and spangled tights.
Those whistling knives of his
are kitchened at night.

(*Poems Four*, 1974)

AT CIRCE'S PLACE

was it want or fear
or both that he felt
as he groaned and took
her helplessly?
He started to change
while grinning with joy
ejaculate, while boars
snuffed in the slops
around her bower.
He couldn't stop
or make change stop,
because of her powers.

(*Iowa Review*, 1973)

POEM

The person who can do
accounts receivable as fast
as steel machines and out-
talk telephones, has wiped
her business lipstick off,
undone her girdle and belts,
and stepped down sighing from
the black quoins of her heels
to be the quiet smiler with
changed eyes. After long-
haired women have unwired
their pencil-pierced buns, it's an
event with pennants when
the Great Falls of emotion say
that beauty is in residence,
grand in her hotel of flesh,
and Venus of the marriage manual,
haloed by a diaphragm,
steps from the shell *Mercenaria*
to her constitutional majesty
in the red world of love.

(*Poems*, 1961)

FOR LISA

May flowers of dirt and
flowers of rocketry both
be in your bunch, love,
when you get married out
beyond my death to you
and the world's wars.
Agreed! Oh she agrees
to anything for laughs,
love, and being danced
to records playing dances.

(*Poems Three*, 1967)

CONSPIRACY OF TWO AGAINST THE WORLD

If I were out of love
and sequence I would turn
the end of love—its death—
knifelike against myself
to cut off my distinction and
rejoin the Commons, maimed.
But love is here!, so by
that contact with the one
oh may I contact all
self-alienated aliens
in Atom City and apply
to join the one big union.
Workers of this world, unite!

(*Poems Three*, 1967)

POEM

It is no wonder that new lovers run
rice gantlets to Niagara Falls
or to some other elephant wonder:
once weightless love finds bodying
in the archaic landscapes of the flesh
it needs proportion in its flow
and goes to public waters. There
it falls asleep unoverwhelmed
while fall sounds shake the panes
of Sweetheart Cottages & Darling Hotel,
and wakes up ordinarily disposed to say:
"I gained ten pounds!", "We never got
to see the Falls!", or, "All is well."

> Oh put the elephant in chains.
> His must is dangerous.
> Three tons of love in pain
> run trumpeting over us.

(*Poems Three*, 1967)

POEM

Flowering balls!,
roses are coming on
in solar systems oh
galactic rose bush. By
tomorrow, given rain,
roses will be out for bees.
It's yours and mine, wild
rose, to open to for love,
its stingers and its rain,
but it is Its always.

(Poems Three, 1967)

UNTITLED POEM

I love the way the heel of my hand feels
as it moves down her spinal column
to the beginning of her ass. She is
a beautiful but also a rich woman, so
we artists and writers pay court to her.
If I really got to the ass I could marry her
and make a million dollars in alimony
after the obligatory divorce. I really like
the way I feel she feels but I could not
put up with her accountants, lawyers, children
 (especially the children) and ex-husbands, but,
the way she holds on, the way her back
seemingly yields and plays at the turn of the curve
of the small of her back where her ass
starts to form harmoniously when we kiss
at one of her fund-raising cocktail parties, oh if I
could explore that territory for a while
I would give up my primitive Marxist philosophy,
my dedication to poverty and hatred of the rich,
and almost become the liberal of her own dreams.

(*Poems Five*, 1983)

COP-SHOOTING: ON A NEWSPAPER PHOTOGRAPH

She just shot him, in the Daily News,
and who can blame her? He,
a sitting cop, and she, a good,
big-hearted woman with a noble flaw:
fury. Cops who have to take their guns
home should see to this: it can
be murder. If the service of the gun
had not been home as a persuader, she
would still be private in her rages, not
as public as that bully Akilles, who,
when shown the metals of good arms,
"at once was moved to use them."

(*Poems Four*, 1974)

TEACHER'S LAMENT

The sidewalk says,
in chalk, that he
loves her. What a joke.

So fall is here
again and school
forces the issue: to sow

at harvest. It sits
the sexes side by side
to learn the mysteries

as if they could. Then
they can drive out
on first cold Friday nights

to learn their first delights,
pay later, and dream love.

(*Poems Four*, 1974)

UNTITLED POEM

What I remember most
about her is her clear eyes
and lips talking all
the time: no conversation,
no screwing. When I tell
her that I'll write a love
poem to her she says Great,
excuse me for a minute,
I have to go to the john.

Did you make the poem.
No.

A red leaf
fell in her hair
and got stuck in it
earlier in the day.

My heart rocked my body asleep that night
but I woke up sweating with terror anyhow
at four o'clock in the morning, for the usual reasons.

(*Poems Four*, 1974)

ABSENT GOOD GIRL, LIFE OF MY MIND

I'm alone in the house.
The wind is outside.
You're in my head.
We look out the window.
A crocus is opening visibly.
We forget dream-fucking you.
I go outside to smell it.
You are there in the flower.
You and the flower can never
know of my love for you two.

(*Poems Four*, 1974)

FOR A LOST GIRL

The skinny girl I never loved and lost, ah how
she pressed against me, how I pressed her so
she disappeared in me, ribs meshed into ribs,
prick into cunt, toes into toes to the heels.
She turned on our pelvic bones and settled in,
locked in my bones in itching sweetness. Then
she fell asleep, smiling. That's how I lost her.
She is the one I walk around with in the way
the marathon dancers used to do it: she
asleep in me, while I dance after a prize.
So when I hear a girl's voice in my mouth
or see another's eyelids on my eyes when I'm asleep,
it's her, so I come to her in losses of wet dreams
the wrong way, outward, not inward to herself.
It is by this love that I rationalize myself
to myself, in hopes of the death of first self-love.

(*Poems Four*, 1974)

TRANSFORMATION

She's changed, my six-foot
bucktoothed student in braces,
pleated skirts and knee-socks,
the way that some birds change
their plumage and songs in spring.
Her hair's down, her awkwardness
and braces are gone, and man,
does she dress! Slinky! He must
have been some quickening lover, that
married professor I saw her with
a couple of times downtown, or else he was
merely a tool of her changes, because she said,
"I'm gonna find myself a nice boy
now and settle down." Luck!

(*Poems Five*, 1983)

GLAD AT THE COLD (1955)

The live storm went through last night
and blew away fall. Many leaves
are in the gutters of this street
which doesn't even have a tree. I'm glad
at the cold because that wind
is cold enough to drive you back to town
the way the homeless lungers must go back
to the pneumonia wards in Bellevue Hospital.
I think I am your ultimate shelter too,
so, shiver in your suntan for a while
until the pipes freeze in your summer place
and then come back to town: there will
be some warmth here with me. When
certain November comes around with probable you
you should be solid, laughing with health,
and sad at the cold and the fading suntan.
Oh may we snug out winter in this dark
city apartment, almost underground. Then,
etiolated in spring, oh you can go
bloom in the countryside again, since I
can't even try to keep you from the sunlight.

(*Poems Five*, 1983)

APOLOGY (TO THE MUSE)

I'm so unaware of what
is going on around me that
I like to watch the brief lives
of the birds: they look around
before they take a seed because
they're always there at present,
self-accounted for in their fears,
hungers and the necessaries
of their rites, whereas I
do not see approaching cars
forget dinner and my address
and realize your beauty
only after you have made a pass
and gone away, saying, "Oh well."

(*Poems Five*, 1983)

UNTITLED POEM

I'm waiting for you, but not purely.
I'm not all waiting the way a dog
outside a supermarket is all waiting
for his mistress, doing nothing else
but waiting, having nothing else to do.
Oh I have something else I have to do,
I think, and I can make up things to do,
so that I am not all waiting like a dog,
but I am waiting for you, though nor purely.
So come on, come out, wherever you are
or else my impure waiting might change
to pure waiting, or into mad waiting.
I might stop waiting entirely just
when you, as you say, say "I'm coming."

(*Poems Five*, 1983)

PROVINCETOWN *TOTENTANZ*

It's obscene, the way you have a girl's voice
and flirtatious manner in a broken-down old body.
When we stand together on canes at cocktail parties
you say, Let's kiss, nobody kisses anymore,
come on, kiss me, I'll give you AIDS.
Remembering how you felt when you were fifty,
I could get a hard-on if I could get a hard-on
so I send you off to get another zombie.
Then we can dance together later, drunk.
six-legged, bones to bones, we'll knock 'em dead,
you, the ancient flapper, me, who looks like death,
as figures in the comic strip The Plague Years
for these kids who never knew what it was like to kiss
everybody at the party!, regardless of the sex.

(*Poems Six*, 1989)

POEM

After your first poetry reading
I shook hands with you
and got a hard-on. Thank you.
We know that old trees
can not feel a thing
when the green tips burst
through the tough bark in spring,
but that's the way it felt,
that's the Objective Correlative
between us poets, love:
a wholly unexpected pain
of something new breaking out
with something old about it
like your new radical poems,
those audible objects of love
breaking out through nerves
as you sweated up on stage,
going raw into painful air
for everyone to know.

(*Poems Six*, 1989)

ON A MYTH.
ON A CONVENTIONAL WISDOM

Who has more fun in bed, men or women,
Zeus asked Tiresias, who had been both,
and when Tiresias answered, Women, of course,
Zeus got so mad he blinded him, he broke his bones,
he sent him back down to earth as a Theban seer.
and you know what happened to Thebes: Pfft!

It was a classic masculine response: We men
have less fun than women in bed, we can't
have children, we can't even have the pleasure
of suckling them, so we go around with empty looks
on our faces looking for excitement, ecstasy, revenge,
we blind people, we break their bones, we destroy
    Thebes.

This is the classic masculine response, this
is the conventional wisdom, this, we hope, is the myth.

(*Poems Six*, 1989)

ON A SUMMER GODDESS WHO SHOULD
BE NAMELESS

There are two things you have
to worry about about her.
She opens up for you
and she closes up on you,
but you shouldn't worry
too much about it because
this is the way she is
and this is the way you are:
You just shouldn't mention her name.
She loves you in her own way
and you love her in your own way
but you should never call her an ox.
If you call a woman an ox you're dead,
so what do you say about a goddess?
She might keep you alive, and in her own hell,
so you have to sweet-talk her to death, your own,
and call her by all sorts of names
like ox-eye daisy, dog-dayes-eye,
gold flower, white flower, clear flower,
Chrysanthemum leucanthemum or *Bellis perennis*!,
anything to avoid it, the name

of the ox-eyed goddess, the one
whose name begins with an H,
has two letters, E and R, and ends in an A,
you know the one I mean,
the one who comes on Midsummer Night
protected by and running that dog,
Sirius, to oversee the crisis
of opening and closing time:
that's when the flowers start
to bloom themselves to death
so that their seeds can blow away
and start up someplace else,
so watch it: do right by her
and her daisies. Beware the dog:
He's called Rusty or Red Dog
or else Blackie or Black Dog because:
If he looks down at you
out of one of his red eyes
if she happens to ask him to
as they swing by overhead,
you and yours and your whole countryside
will be wholly burnt up to black ashes.

(*Poems Six*, 1989)

NIGHT SCENE BEFORE COMBAT

There are trucks going down our street tonight
in convoy. The window rattles. There are lights
going on and off in the sky
beyond the suburbs, accompanied
by noises that sound like thunder.
I should be with them but
I try to get some sleep
with you. Did you know
that Metaphor means Truck
in Modern Greek? Truck. Carryall.
It figures. As William Blake said,
Eternity is in love with us
creations of time, and you *know*
about love, not just the weapons and battles,
but the problems of supply, logistics,
of getting the material to the front,
to the precise point of fire, in trucks,
at that point of place, at this point in time,
when the lights are flashing on and off
and what might sound like thunder is
not thunder, not thunder at all.
I should go downstairs and join

my outfit, I should get back
to the truck I left idling
by the curb, but I turn to you
for one last time in sleep, love,
before I put my uniform back on,
check my piece, and say So long.

(*Poems Six*, 1989)

DRUNKEN MEMORIES OF ANNE SEXTON

The first and last time I met
my ex-lover Anne Sexton was at
a protest poetry reading against
some anti-constitutional war in Asia
when some academic son of a bitch,
to test her reputation as a drunk,
gave her a beer glass full of wine
after our reading. She drank
it all down while staring me
full in the face and then said
"I don't care what you think,
you know," as if I was
her ex-what, husband, lover,
what? and just as I
was just about to say I
loved her, I was, what,
was, interrupted by my beautiful enemy
Galway Kinnell, who said to her
"Just as I was told, your eyes,
you have one blue, one green"

and there they were, the two
beautiful poets, staring at
each others' beautiful eyes
as I drank the lees of her wine.

(*Poems Seven*, 2001)

NOTE OF QUITS

Don't walk barefoot in the bathroom.
There was someone in the mirror who I killed.
God bless your hair-brush. God bless you.
Though I swept up as best I could,
there might be slivers of revenge left underfoot,
so watch out for intrusion, love: be shod.

(*Poems Seven*, 2001)

PROTHALAMION OF QUANTUM MECHANICS AND ASTROPHYSICS AGAINST THE TEXT "PHILOSOPHIA BIOU KUBERNETES" (PHILOSOPHY THE GUIDE OF LIFE)

from Part I: The Stutter of Quanta

. . .

　　　　You part your thing
　　　　at me
　　　　and wave your part.
You part your part
and wave your wave
at me.
You wave and part
and part and wave
your thing and part,
waving,

　　　　　　　　at me.

I withdraw inconsummate
if you are approximate,

I am empty, I
am in val-
id, I represent no
knowable abstraction if
I love you only because
you have no definite figure.
My love is incomplete in theory.
My love is uncertain in principle.
Whether you matter or
do not matter, whether
you are real or false,
I either love or am the law.
Therefore I will be as constant
as Max Planck's Constant in constant,
though divided in this farce
by two pis or more, more.

Part II. Dirge/Scherzo

In dreams I think
you are behaving like
my model universe
but know that you're
not sensible and that

you have a cloudy past,
no definite figure,
and are infinitely multiple,
divisible eternally,
but you are everything to me
so I want all of you
to be (Please be)
(considered as) my only one,
I want all of you
to be my only one.

What can I say as we go away
from one another, you and I,
except that I am not thoughtful,
that I am insensitive and imperceptive.
I don't even know if I could hope
that you and I could get together again,
or else slow down and find stability,
or simply go away forever, fast,
and leave me saying empty verse
out to an emptying universe:

   Oh I don't know where you're going,
I don't know where you're at.
I don't know where you come from

or if you're coming back,
so tell me how I love you.

from Part III: Antennae of Astrophysics and The
    End of Optics

. . .
so we live in one another's pasts,
you and I, and go into our own
futures all alone. We are always
moving apart and getting larger
and looking smaller, you in your
beautiful red shift, and me,
bug-eyed, observatory, shelled,
waving my antennae out at you
and flying away. I have my doubts
that I'm your metamorphic worm,
yolked in your egg of unknowability
and flying timewise to be born or burned.

(*Poems Seven*, 2001)

From an

INTERVIEW WITH ALAN DUGAN BY KEITH
ALTHAUS THAT APPEARED IN *NORTHWEST
REVIEW* IN 1982 . . .

DUGAN: Yes, both visual art, plastic art, and music. They're highly important to me. I have the feeling that a lot of my poetry is very visually oriented. I've written poems in response to my wife's work and other artists' work; but on the other hand, one of the other borders of poetry is music and in my verse, sometimes unconsciously, sometimes consciously, I always kind of count and I'm always kind of musical, so in that sense, I'm rather a formalist in my approach to writing verse.

ALTHAUS: I think you're terribly musical, at least my reading of it. I always read them as lyrical, no matter how they're broken on the page or whether the rhymes are hidden or not. They seem extremely musical.

DUGAN: I love to rhyme, I love to count, but I figure in a poem that the person who reads it, who hears it, doesn't have to know, so I'm kind of sneaky about that.

ALTHAUS: Varying it, you mean?

DUGAN: Yeah. You don't have to rhyme at the end of lines and you don't have to count lines, but I like to do both things. But the painting thing is interesting—I could say something; I don't know whether it'd work on tape, but behind you there is a silkscreen of a yellow pick-up truck which was done by my wife, Judith Shahn, and it's an empty yellow pick-up truck, nobody in it, so what I did was to make a reprise, a reply to her silkscreen. . . . The poem is on top. . . . This is not going to work in terms of the tape, so . . . that's an empty yellow pick-up truck, done by my wife, right?

Dear Judy, Thank you for your silkscreen print of the
empty yellow pick-up truck license X71-04 Now I can
dream the absent young bearded driver's American Dream.

He has a beautiful girl riding shot-gun, a Doberman
pinscher in the truckbed and a broom upright in its
socket. For out west I add a gun rack in the rear
window. Love, Dugan

(*Northwest Review*, 1982)

PERMISSIONS AND SOURCES

The poems included in *Love Poems* were chosen from *Poems Seven: New and Complete Poetry* by Alan Dugan, and are included here by permission of Seven Stories Press.

Two additional poems and a short interview excerpt were supplied by the poet Keith Althaus.

INDEX